40 Top Questions About Islam

40 سؤالا حول الإسلام

[إنجليزي - English]

Collected by : Ali Ateeq Al-Dhaheri

2013 - 1434

Introduction

All praise is due to Allah. We praise Him, seek for His help and forgiveness and we seek refuge with Him from evils of our souls and our misdeeds. No one can mislead whosoever Allah guides and none can guide whosoever Allah causes to go astray.

I testify that there is no deity worthy of worship except Allah alone. He has no partner. I also testify that Muhammad(saws) is His slave and Messenger.

In this work I collected 40 common Questions and answers about Islam from different sources.

It can guide you to understand Islam and find answers to your questions . it contains many subjects about Islam like : Allah, Muslims, prophet Muhammad (Peace be upon him) , Jesus (PB☐H, pillars of Islam , Jihad, polygamy, women ..etc.

I seek ALLAH to guide us to the straightway, the way of those, on whom ALLAH has

Bestowed grace .

1-What is Islam?

The word "Islam" means peace and submission. Peace means to be at peace with yourself and your surroundings and submission means submission to the will of God. A broader meaning of the word "Islam" is to achieve peace by submitting to the will of God.

This is a unique religion with a name which signifies a moral attitude and a way of life. Judaism takes its name from the tribe of Juda, Christianity from Jesus Christ, Buddhism from Goutam Buddha and Hinduism from Indus River. However, Muslims derive their identity from the message of Islam, rather than the person of Muhammed (Peace be upon him), thus should not be called "Muhammadans".

2- Who is Allah?

Allah is the Arabic word for "one God". Allah is not God of Muslims only. He is God of all creations, because He is their Creator and Sustainer.

3-Does Allah look like us?

No, Allah is perfect. He is not like any of His creations. A Muslim does not say a single thing about Allah other than what Allah says about Himself. Allah is Perfect and Unique.

4-What is the Kabah?

The Kabah is the place of worship, which God commanded Abraham and Ishmael to build over four thousand years ago. The building was constructed of stone on what many believe was the original site of a sanctuary established by Adam. God commanded

Abraham to summon all mankind to visit this place, and when pilgrims go there today they say 'At Thy service, O Lord', in response to Abraham's summons.

5- Who is a Muslim?

The word "Muslim" means one who submits to the will of God. This is done by declaring that "there is no god except one God and Muhammad is the messenger of God." In a broader sense, anyone who willingly submits to the will of God is a Muslim. Thus, all the prophets preceding the prophet Muhammad are considered Muslims. The Quran specifically mentions Abraham who lived long before Moses and Christ that, "he was not a Jew or a Christian but a Muslim," because, he had submitted to the will of God. Thus there are Muslims who are not submitting at all to the will of God and there are Muslims who are doing their best to live an Islamic life. One cannot judge Islam by looking at those individuals who have a Muslim name but in their actions, they are not living or behaving as Muslims. The extent of being a Muslim can be according to the degree to which one is submitting to the will of God, in his beliefs and his actions.

6- Who was Muhammad? (Peace be upon him)

In brief, Muhammad (Peace be upon him) was born in a noble tribe of Mecca in Arabia in the year 570 AD. His ancestry goes back to Prophet Ishmael (Peace be upon him), son of Prophet Abraham (Peace be upon him). His father died before his birth and his mother died when he was six. He did not attend a formal school since he was raised first by a nurse as it was the custom those days, and then by his grandfather and uncle. As a young man, he was known as a righteous person who used to meditate in a cave. At age 40, he was given the prophethood when the angel, Gabriel, appeared in the cave. Subsequently, the revelations came over 23 years and were compiled in the form of a book called the Quran which Muslims consider as the final and the last word of God. The Quran has been preserved, unchanged, in its original form and confirms the truth in the Torah, the psalms and the Gospel. (1)

7- How did Muhammad (peace be upon him) become a prophet and a messenger of God?

At the age of 40, while engaged in a meditative retreat, Muhammad (peace be upon him) received his first revelation from God through the Angel Gabriel. This revelation, which continued for twenty-three years, is known as the Quran.

As soon as he began to recite the words he heard from Gabriel, and to preach the truth that God had revealed to him, he and his small group of followers suffered bitter persecution, which grew so fierce that in the year 622 God gave them the command to emigrate. This event, the Hijrah, 'migration', in which they left Makkah for the city of Madinah some 260 miles to the north, marks the beginning of the Muslim calendar.

After several years, the Prophet (peace be upon him) and his followers were able to return to Makkah, where they forgave their enemies and established Islam definitively. Before the Prophet (peace be upon him) died at the age of 63, the greater part of Arabia was Muslim, and within a century of his death Islam had spread to Spain in the West and as Far East as China.

8- Do Muslims worship Muhammad? (Peace be upon him)

No. Muslims do not worship Muhammad (Peace be upon him) or any other prophets. Muslims believe in all prophets including Adam, Noah, Abraham, David, Solomon, Moses and Jesus. Muslims believe that Muhammad (Peace be upon him) was the last of the prophets. They believe that God alone is to be worshiped, not any human being.

1-Khan,The personality of Allah's last messenger , p (17-34)

9-What is the Quran?

The Quran is a record of the exact words revealed by God through the Angel Gabriel to the Prophet Muhammad (peace be upon him). It was memorized by Muhammad (peace be upon him) and then dictated to his companions, and written down by scribes, who crosschecked it during his lifetime. Not one word of its 114 Surahs, has been changed over the centuries, so that the Quran is in every detail the unique and miraculous text which was revealed to Muhammad (peace be upon him) fourteen centuries ago.

10-What is the Quran about?

The Quran, the last revealed Word of God, is the prime source of every Muslim's faith and practice. It deals with all the subjects which concern us as human beings: wisdom, doctrine, worship, and law, but its basic theme is the relationship between God and His creatures. At the same time, it provides guidelines for a just society, proper human conduct and an equitable economic system.

11-Are there any other sacred sources?

Yes, the Sunnah, the practice and example of the Prophet (peace be upon him), is the second authority for Muslims. A Hadith is a reliably transmitted report of what the Prophet (peace be upon him) said, did, or approved. Belief in the Sunnah is part of the Islamic faith.

Examples of the Prophet's sayings

The Prophet (peace be upon him) said:

'God has no mercy on one who has no mercy for others.'

'None of you truly believes until he wishes for his brother what he wishes for himself.'

'Powerful is not he who knocks the other down, indeed powerful is he who controls himself in a fit of anger.'

(From the Hadith collections of Bukhari, Muslim, Tirmidhi and Baihaqi.)

12-How do we know Islam is the truth?

1- It is the only religion that holds Allah as One, Unique, and Perfect.

2- It is the only religion that believes in the sole worship of Allah, not Jesus, not an idol, and not an

angel, only Allah.
3- The Quran does not contain contradictions.
4- The Quran contains scientific facts, which are 1300 years ahead of their time. The Quran, while revealed 1400 years ago contains scientific facts, which are only now being discovered. It is not in contradiction to science.
5- Allah has challenged the world to produce the like of the Quran. And He says they won't be able to.
6- Prophet Muhammad (peace be upon him) was the most influential man in history. In the book "The 100 most influential men in History", written by non-Muslim, the Prophet Muhammad (peace be upon him) was #1. Prophet Jesus (peace be upon him) was #3. It should be noted that even the Prophet Jesus (peace be upon him) was a prophet sent by Allah.

13-Does Islam tolerate other beliefs?

The Qur'an says:

Allah does not forbid you with regards to those who do not fight you for [your] faith nor drive you out of your homes, from dealing kindly and justly with them; for Allah loves those who are just.
(Qur'an, 60:8)

There is no compulsion in religion. (2:214)

It is one of the functions of Islamic law to protect the privileged status of minorities, and this is why non-

Muslim places of worship have flourished all over the Islamic world. History provides many examples of Muslim tolerance towards other faiths. For example, when the caliph Omar entered Jerusalem in the year 634, he granted amnesty to all and sanctioned freedom of worship to all religious communities in the city. Another example is Muslims who ruled the Spain had such tolerance of other beliefs that the Golden Age of Jewish Civilization flourished under the Muslim rule.

Not only that, Islamic law permits non-Muslim minorities to set up their own courts thus allowing them the autonomy to be judged according to their family law.

14-Do Islam and Christianity have different origins?

Together with Judaism, they go back to the prophet and patriarch Abraham, and their three prophets are directly descended from his sons-Muhammad (peace be upon him) from the eldest, Ishmael, and Moses and Jesus, from Isaac. Abraham established the settlement, which today is the city of Makkah, and built the Kabah towards which all Muslims turn when they pray.

15. What do Muslims think of Jesus? (Peace be upon him)

Muslims think highly of Jesus (peace be upon him) and his worthy mother, Mary. The Quran tells us that Jesus was born of a miraculous birth without a father. "Lo! The likeness of Jesus with Allah is the likeness of Adam. He created him of dust, and then He said unto him: Be and he is" (Quran 3.59). He was given many miracles as a prophet. These include speaking soon after his birth in defense of his mother's piety. God's other gifts to him included healing the blind and the sick, reviving the dead, making a bird out of clay and most importantly, the message he was carrying. These miracles were given to him by God to establish him as a prophet. According to the Quran, he was not crucified but was raised into Heaven. (Quran, Chapter Maryam)

16-"How can you believe in God, when you can't see, hear, touch, smell, taste or even imagine what He is?"

We know from the teachings of Muhammad, peace be upon him, that no one has ever actually seen God - at least not in this lifetime. Nor are we able to use our senses to make some kind of contact with Him. However, we are encouraged in Islam to use our senses and our common sense to recognize that all of this universe could not possibly come into existence on its own. Something had to design it all and then put it into motion. That is beyond our ability to do, yet it is something that we can understand.

We don't have to see an artist to recognize a painting, correct? So, if we see paintings without seeing artists painting them, in the same way, we can believe that Allah created everything without having to see Him (or touch, or hear, etc.).(1)

17- What are the pillars of Islam?

There are five major pillars of Islam which are the articles of faith. These pillars are 1) the belief (Iman) in one God and that Muhammad (P) is His messenger, 2) prayer (Salat) which are prescribed five times a day, 3) fasting (Siyam) which is required in the month of Ramadan, 4) charity (Zakat) which is the poor-due on the wealth of the rich and 5) hajj which is the pilgrimage to Mecca once in a lifetime if one can afford it physically and financially. All the pillars should be of equal height and strength in a building in order to give the building its due shape and proportions. It is not possible that one would do hajj without observing fasting or without practicing regular prayers. Now think of a building which has pillars only. It would not be called a building. In order to make it a building, it has to have a roof, it has to have walls, it has to have doors and windows. These things in Islam are the moral codes of Islam such as honesty, truthfulness, steadfastness and many other human moral qualities. Thus in order to be a Muslim, one should not only be practicing the pillars of Islam but should also have the highest possible attribute for being a good human being. Only then the building is completed and looks beautiful.

18- What is the purpose of worship in Islam?

The purpose of worship in Islam is to be God conscious. Thus the worship, whether it is prayer, fasting, or charity, is a means to achieve God consciousness so that when one becomes conscious of God, in thought and in action, he is in a better position to receive His bounties both in this world and the hereafter.

19- Do Muslims believe in the hereafter?

God is Just and manifest His justice, He established the system of accountability. Those who do good will be rewarded and those who do wrong will be punished accordingly. Thus, He created Heaven and Hell and there are admission criteria for both. Muslims believe that the present life is a temporary one. It is a test and if we pass the test, we will be given a life of permanent pleasure in the company of good people in Heaven.

20- Will the good actions of the non-believers be wasted?

No. The Quran clearly says that, "anyone who has an atom's worth of goodness will see it and anyone who has done an atom's worth of evil will also see it" (Quran 99:7- 8).
By that it is meant that those who are non- believers but have done good will be rewarded in this world for their good deed. On the other hand, those who do good if they are Muslims, they will be rewarded not only in this world but also in the world hereafter. However, the final Judgment is up to God himself. (Quran 2:62)

1-www:knowingallah.com

21- What is the dress code for Muslims?

Islam emphasizes modesty. No person should be perceived as a sex object. There are certain guidelines both for men and women that their dress should neither be too thin nor too tight to reveal body forms. For men, they must at least cover the area from the knee to navel and for women, their dress should cover all areas except the hands and face.

22- What are the dietary prohibitions in Islam?

Muslims are told in the Quran not to eat pork or pork products, meat of the animals who died before being slaughtered or the carnivorous animals (as they eat dead animals), nor drink blood or intoxicants such as wine or use any illicit drugs.

23- What is Jihad?

The word "Jihad" means struggle, or to be specific, striving in the cause of God. Any struggle done in day-to-day life to please God can be considered Jihad. One of the highest levels of Jihad is to stand up to a tyrant and speak a word of truth. Control of the self from wrong doings is also a great Jihad. One of the forms of Jihad is to take up arms in defense of Islam or a Muslim country when Islam is attacked. This kind of Jihad has to be declared by the religious leadership or by a Muslim head of state who is following the Quran and Sunnah.

24- What is the Islamic Year?

The Islamic year started from the migration (Hijra) of Prophet Muhammad (P) from Mecca to Medina in 622 AD. It is a lunar year of 354 days. The first month is called Muharram. 1996 AD is in Islamic year 1416 AH.

25- What are the major Islamic festivals?

Idul Fitre, marks the end of fasting in the month of Ramadan and is celebrated with public prayers, feasts and exchange of gifts. Idul Adha marks the end of the Hajj or the annual pilgrimage to Mecca. After the public prayers, those who can afford, sacrifice a lamb or a goat to signify Prophet Abraham's obedience to God, shown by his readiness to sacrifice his son Ishmael.

26- What is Sharia?

Sharia is the comprehensive Muslim law derived from two sources, a) the Quran b) the Sunnah or traditions of Prophet Muhammad (Peace be upon him). It covers every aspect of daily individual and collective living. The purpose of Islamic laws are protection of individuals' basic human rights to include right to life, property, political and religious freedom and safeguarding the rights of women and minorities. The low crime rate in Muslim societies is due to the application of the Islamic laws. (1)

1-www:Islamichotline.com

27- Was Islam spread by the sword?

According to the Quran, "There is no compulsion in religion" (2:256), thus, no one can be forced to become a Muslim. While it is true that in many places where Muslim armies went to liberate people or the land, they did carry the sword as that was the weapon used at that time. However, Islam did not spread by the sword because in many places where there are Muslims now, in the Far East like Indonesia, in China, and many parts of Africa, there are no records of any Muslim armies going there. To say that Islam was spread by the sword would be to say that Christianity was spread by guns, F-16's and atomic bombs, etc., which is not true. Christianity spread by the missionary works of Christians. Ten-percent of all Arabs are Christians. The "Sword of Islam" could not convert all the non-Muslim minorities in Muslim countries. In India, where Muslims ruled for 700 years, they are still a minority. In the U.S.A., Islam is the fastest growing religion and has 6 million followers without any sword around.

28- Does Islam promote violence and terrorism?

No. Islam is religion of peace and submission and stresses on the sanctity of human life. A verse in the Quran says, [Chapter 5, verse 32], that "anyone who saves one life, it is as if he has saved the whole of mankind and anyone who has killed another person (except in lieu of murder or mischief on earth) it is as if he has killed the whole of mankind." Islam condemns all the violence which happened in the Crusades, in Spain, in WW II, or by acts of people like the Rev. Jim Jones, David Koresh, Dr. Baruch Goldstein, or the atrocities committed in Bosnia by the Christian Serbs. Anyone who is doing violence is not practicing his religion at that time. However, sometimes violence is a human response of oppressed people as it happens in Palestine. Although this is wrong, they think of this as a way to get attention. There is a lot of terrorism and violence in areas where there is no Muslim presence. For example, in Ireland, South Africa, Latin America, and Sri Lanka. Sometimes the violence is due to a struggle between those who have with those who do not have, or between those who are oppressed with those who are oppressors. We need to find out why people become terrorists. Unfortunately, the Palestinians who are doing violence are called terrorists, but not the armed Israeli settlers when they do the same sometimes even against their own people. As it turned out to be in the Oklahoma City bombing, sometime Muslims are prematurely blamed even if the terrorism is committed by non-Muslims. Sometimes those who want Peace and those who oppose Peace can be of the same religion.

29- What is "Islamic Fundamentalism"?

There is no concept of "Fundamentalism" in Islam. The western media has coined this term to brand those Muslims who wish to return to the basic fundamental principles of Islam and mould their lives accordingly. Islam is a religion of moderation and a practicing God fearing Muslim can neither be a fanatic nor an extremist.

30-Is Islamic marriage like Christian marriage?

In Islam, marriage is one of the most sacred bonds that two humans can forge. In addition, a marriage in Islam is also practical involving legal agreement and contractual obligations which spouses mutually agreed upon.

According to Islam, no Muslim girl or boy can be forced to marry against their will. Parents are to play a proactive and active role in suggesting potential spouses, but not to impose a decision upon their children.

31- Does Islam promote polygamy?

No, polygamy in Islam is a permission not an injunction. Historically, all the prophets except Jesus, who was not married, had more than one wife. For Muslim men to have more than one wife is a permission which is given to them in the Quran, not to satisfy lust, but for the welfare of the widows and the orphans of the wars. In the pre-Islamic period, men used to have many wives. One person had 11 wives and when he became Muslim, he asked the Prophet Muhammad (Peace be upon him), "What should I do with so many wives?" and he said, "Divorce all except the four." The Quran says, "you can marry 2 or 3 and up to 4 women if you can be equally just with each of them" (4:3). Since it is very difficult to be equally just with all wives, in practice, most of the Muslim men do not have more than one wife. Prophet Muhammad (Peace be upon him) himself from age 24 to 50 was married to only one woman, Khadija. In the western society, some men who have one wife have many extramarital affairs. Thus, a survey was published in "U.S.A. Today" (April 4, 1988 Section D) which asked 4,700 mistresses what they would like their status to be. They said that "they preferred being a second wife rather than the 'other woman' because they did not have the legal rights, nor did they have the financial equality of the legally married wives, and it appeared that they were being used by these men."

32- Does Islam oppress women?

No. On the contrary, Islam elevated the status of women 1,400 years ago by giving them the right to divorce, the right to have financial independence and support and the right to be identified as dignified women (Hijab) when in the rest of the world, including Europe, women had no such rights. Women are equal to men in all acts of piety (Quran 33:32). Islam allows women to keep their maiden name after marriage, their earned money and spend it as they wish, and ask men to be their protector as women on the street can be molested. Prophet Muhammad (Peace be upon him) told Muslim men, "the best among you is the one who is best to his family." Not Islam, but some Muslim men, do oppress women today. This is because of their cultural habits or their ignorance about their religion.

33- Is Islam intolerant of other religious minorities?

Islam recognizes the rights of the minority. To ensure their welfare and safety, Muslim rulers initiated a tax (Jazia) on them. Prophet Muhammad (Peace be upon him) forbade Muslim armies to destroy churches and synagogues. Caliph Umer did not even allow them to pray inside a church. Jews were welcomed and flourished in Muslim Spain even when they were persecuted in the rest of Europe. They consider that part of their history as the Golden Era. In Muslim countries, Christians live in prosperity, hold government positions and attend their church. However, the same religious tolerance is not always available to Muslim minorities as seen in the past during Spanish inquisition and the crusades, or as seen now by the events in Bosnia, Israel and India. Muslims do recognize that sometimes the actions of a ruler does not reflect the teachings of his religion.

34- What is the Islamic view on-

a. Dating and Premarital sex:
Islam does not approve of intimate mixing of the sexes, and forbids premarital or extramarital sex. Islam encourages marriage as a shield to such temptations and as a means of having mutual love, mercy and peace.

b. Abortion:
Islam considers abortion as murder and does not permit it except to save the mother's life (Quran 17:23-31, 6:15 1).

c. Homosexuality and AIDS:
Islam categorically opposes homosexuality and considers it a sin. However, Muslim physicians are advised to care for AIDS patients with compassion just as they would for other patients.

d. Euthanasia and Suicide:
Islam is opposed to both suicide and euthanasia. Muslims do not believe in heroic measures to prolong the misery in a terminally ill patient.

e. Organ transplantation:

Islam stresses upon saving lives (Quran 5:32); thus, transplantation in general would be considered permissible in necessity provided a donor consent is available. The sale of the organ is not allowed.

35- How should Muslims treat Jews and Christians?

The Quran calls them "People of the Book", i.e., those who received Divine scriptures before Muhammad (Peace be upon him) . Muslims are told to treat them with respect and justice and do not fight with them unless they initiate hostilities or ridicule their faith. The
Muslims ultimate hope is that they all will join them in worshipping one God and submit to His will.

"Say (O Muhammad): O people of the Book (Jews and Christians) come to an agreement between us and you, that we shall worship none but Allah, and that we shall take no partners with Him, and none of us shall take others for Lords beside Allah. And if they turn away, then say: Bear witness that we are those who have surrendered (unto Him)." (Quran 3:64)

What about Hindus, Bahai, Buddhists and members of other religions?
They should also be treated with love, respect, and understanding to make them recipients of Invitations to Islam.

36-How does Islam guarantee human rights?

Freedom of conscience is laid down by the Qur'an itself: 'There is no compulsion in religion'. (2:256)

The life and property of all citizens in an Islamic state are considered sacred whether a person is Muslim or not.

'O mankind! We created you from a single soul, male and female, and made you into nations and tribes, so that you may come to know one another. Truly, the most honored of you in Allah's sight is the greatest of you in piety. Allah is All-Knowing, All-Aware. (49:13)

37-Why is the family so important to Muslims?

The family is the foundation of Islamic society. The peace and security offered by a stable family unit is greatly valued, and seen as essential for the spiritual growth of its members. A harmonious social order is created by the existence of extended families; children are treasured, and rarely leave home until the time they marry.

38-How do Muslims treat the elderly?

In the Islamic world there are no old people's homes. The strain of caring for one's parents in this most difficult time of their lives is considered an honor and blessing, and an opportunity for great spiritual growth. God asks that we not only pray for our parents, but act with limitless compassion, remembering that when we were helpless children they preferred us to themselves. Mothers are particularly honored: the Prophet (Peace be upon him) taught that 'Paradise lies at the feet of mothers'.

When they reach old age, Muslim parents are treated mercifully, with the same kindness and selflessness. In Islam, serving one's parents is a duty second only to prayer, and it is their right to expect it.

The Qur'an says: 'Your Lord has commanded that you worship none but Him, and be kind to parents. If either or both of them reach old age with you, do not say 'Uff' to them or chide them, but speak to them in terms of honor and kindness. Treat them with humility, and say, 'My Lord! Have mercy on them, for they cared for me when I was little'. (17:23-4)

39-What about food?

Although much simpler than the dietary law followed by Jews and the early Christians, the code which Muslims observe forbids the consumption of pig meat or any kind of intoxicating drink. The Prophet Muhammad (peace be upon him) taught that 'your body has rights over you', and the consumption of wholesome food and the leading of a healthy lifestyle are seen as religious obligations. The Prophet (peace be upon him) said: 'Ask God for certainty [of faith] and well-being; for after certainty, no one is given any gift better than health!'

40-Can anyone become a Muslim?

Yes anyone can. There are two declarations, which are necessary:

1- To bear witness that no one deserves to be worshiped except Allah.

2- To bear witness that Prophet Muhammad (peace be upon him) is the Messenger of Allah.

This makes a person Muslim. But it should be said in Arabic. Next a person takes a shower is recommendable .

Then what?

After a person becomes Muslim s/he is taught about prayers, fasting, alms to the poor, and pilgrimage. These are the pillars of Islam.

Then what?

Muslims are brothers and sisters. A Muslim should love for his brother or sister what s/he loves for him/herself. Allah's wealth does not run out and Allah can provide for us all. We pray for each other, and love each other, and love for our brothers and sisters what we love for ourselves. (1)

1-www: Islamicfinder.org

References

Discover Islam ,complmenty copy by : shekka Hind Al-Maktoum . U.A.E

This message is for you ,by :Mahmoud Murad , cooperative office for call and guidance .K.S.A

The true religion of god Dr P, Philips, zaid center for new Muslims . U.A.E.

The principles of Islam, by:Hmoud Al-lahim, cooperative office for call and guidance .K.S.A

The personality of Allah s last messenger , by; abdul Waheed Kahan ,IIPH .

Index

Introduction   2

1. What is Islam?   3

2. Who is Allah?   3

3-Does Allah look like us? 3

4-What is the Kabah?   3

5. Who is a Muslim?   3

6. Who was Muhammad?   4

7-How did Muhammad (peace be upon him) become a prophet and a messenger of God? 4

8- Do Muslims worship Muhammad? 4

9-What is the Quran?   5
10-What is the Quran about? 5

11-Are there any other sacred sources? 5

12-How do we know Islam is the truth? 5

13-Does Islam tolerate other beliefs? 6

14-Do Islam and Christianity have different origins? 6

15. What do Muslims think of Jesus?   6

16-"How can you believe in God, when you can't see
6

17- What are the pillars of Islam?   7

18. What is the purpose of worship in Islam?   7

19. Do Muslims believe in the hereafter?   7

20. Will the good actions of the non-believers be wasted? 7

21- What is the dress code for Muslims?   8

22. What are the dietary prohibitions in Islam? 8

23. What is Jihad?   8

24. What is the Islamic Year?   8

25. What are the major Islamic festivals?   8

26. What is Sharia? 8

27. Was Islam spread by the sword? 9

28. Does Islam promote violence and terrorism? 9

29. What is "Islamic Fundamentalism"? 9

30- Is Islamic marriage like Christian marriage? 10

31. Does Islam promote polygamy? 10

32. Does Islam oppress women? 10

33- Is Islam intolerant of other religious minorities? 10

34. What is the Islamic view on ? 11

35. How should Muslims treat Jews and Christians? 11

36- How does Islam guarantee human rights? 12

37-Why is the family so important to Muslims?
12

38-How do Muslims treat the elderly?
12

39-What about food?
13

40-Can anyone become a Muslim?
13

Reverences
14

Index
15

www.ingramcontent.com/pod-product-compliance
Lightning Source LLC
LaVergne TN
LVHW010424070526
838199LV00064B/5412